TARRAGONA
HUMAN • HERITAGE

TARRAGONA
HUMAN • HERITAGE

PHOTOGRAPHY BY **RICARD PLA, JORDI PUIG AND PERE VIVAS** TEXT BY **CARLES MARQUÈS**

TRIANGLE ▼ POSTALS

ROMAN TARRACO: WORLD HERITAGE SITE

"TARRACO TARRACONENSIUM OPUS"
TARRAGONA, WORK OF THE TARRACO PEOPLE

T arragona is much more than Rome. It was the first Roman city outside the Italic peninsula and nearby islands, and capital of the Tarraconense or Citerior region, the largest province. The city, however, is much more than the monuments that the Empire left behind, and which led to the ancient Tarraco being declared a World Heritage Site by UNESCO in 2000. Despite the obvious artistic and architectural interest, which is more than sufficient reason to visit it, Tarragona represents, above all else, a human heritage, the people. Perhaps the same could be said, or perhaps not, of any city, but in this case it is especially true, as you could see for yourselves in the crowded street festivals and activities that mark out the city's life throughout the year.

It is a fact that Tarraco, as the repeated phrase of Pliny goes, is *Scipionum Opus*, work of the Scipios; but it is no less true that since then, and until what is today their 23rd century, it has been made by the people who live and have lived in it. And from people, from what they do, arises another, intangible heritage, that of the culture, festival and language, equally as worthy of recognition as that of the stones.

CISSA, THE IBERIAN SETTLEMENT OF THE COSSETANS

Before the Romans, the lands of Camp de Tarragona were already populated in prehistoric times, as the excavations of Boella and Canonja show. And in the lower part of the city there had been one of the most important Iberian cities in what today is Catalonia. It belonged to the Cossetan tribe and its name was Cissa.

OVER 2200 YEARS "AB URBE CONDITA", SINCE THE FOUNDING OF THE CITY

Gnaeus Scipio belonged to an illustrious family of Roman soldiers. After disembarking at Empúries to fight against the Carthaginian Asdrubal, he headed south, where he met up with his brother Publius Cornelius. When he defeated the Carthaginian troops, in 218 BC, he left a military base in what is today Tarragona. It was a strategic refuge, with a port and excellent communication with the interior of the peninsula. The two Scipio brothers have given their name, popularly but mistakenly to the Torre dels Escipions, a funerary monument dating from the 1st century AD. The two figures are representations of the funerary god Atius.

The city founded as an encampment soon became the epicentre of the Romanisation of the Peninsula and one of the most important economic, cultural and social focal points of the Mediterranean. The *Colonia Iulia Urbs Triumphalis Tarraco* also became the *de facto* capital of the entire Empire, since the Emperor Augustus lived there for two years while he battled with the Cantabrians and Asturians.

The city reached its maximum age of splendour in the 1st century AD, with the Flavian dynasty: the Emperor Vespasian had the Provincial Forum built there and his son Domitian, the Circus, to which was added the Amphitheatre in the 2nd century AD. Tarraco is one of the few cities in the Roman world that had three buildings for entertainment. The third was the Theatre, from the Augustine period, abandoned in the 2nd century AD. The lower part was left uninhabited in the 4th century, and Tarraco reduced to the old monumental area.

THE BIGGEST AND LONGEST WALL

What in the beginning must have been a wooden fenced stockade became, at the end of the 3rd century, the Muralla, the wall, the oldest and largest monument of the Peninsula: and totally Roman at that. Do not look for Iberian or mythical origins in the megalithic blocks that support the upper blocks of stone. Everything, including the 12 metres height, the width between 4 and 6 metres, and the length, which was about 4 kilometres, of which more than one is still standing, is the result of the inventiveness and architecture of Rome.

The Muralla, described in texts and poems, photographed and even sung about, is one of the most representative and represented parts of Tarragona. In 1933 the Archaeological Path was opened at its feet, which runs parallel to the Falsa Braga, the work of British engineers during the War of Succession. Only one of the main doors of the Muralla has been preserved, the Socors doorway, close to the Minerva Tower, even though another six smaller doors, or narrow gateways, still survive.

Another path, not so archaeological, extends beyond the Muralla, along the old parapet walk. From here you can look out over the houses of the Part Alta, alongside the flat roofs, the clothes hung out to dry, the voices and the smells: of living history.

THE MINERVA, CAPISCOL AND ARCHBISHOP TOWERS

A series of towers completed the Roman fortress, in the true sense of the word, of which three remain. That of Minerva, or Sant Magí, is the one that preserves its original form the most. On the upper part, you can see a fragment of the relief of Minerva, in which you can make out the feet, tunic and a shield with a wolf's head, attribute of the selfsame Goddess, protector of the arts, war and civil freedom, three spheres that may seem paradoxical seen together.

The tower hides, and to a part that you will not see, the oldest Roman inscription on the Peninsula, dedicated to the Goddess. It also hides a series of small, sculpted heads on stones, made to frighten away the enemy. The Iberians cut off and hung up the heads of their enemies, and the Romans copied this custom, but in stone. They are not easy to find, but you can play at discovering them.

The form that the Archbishop Tower currently takes, otherwise known as the tower of Pavorde (an old ecclesiastical dignitary), is medieval. The Capiscol Tower, which also owes its name to a late dignitary, also has a double name, the tower of the Seminary.

THE OLDEST MUSEUM OF ANTIQUITY

The National Archaeological Museum of Tarragona, MNAT, is the oldest in Catalonia in its speciality. It was built in the mid-19th century, and its first home was in the Town Hall, in the Plaça de la Font. In 1960 it was moved to the current building, which due to its appearance seems to have been transported from the original Roman Tarraco and which is built over a section of the Muralla. The MNAT includes the Necropolis and the villas of Centcelles and Munts. Among the items it houses feature the best collection of mosaics in Catalonia, some of them so impressive such as the Mosaic of the Medusa, from the 2nd century AD, which has come to be a symbol, a "coat of arms" of Tarragona, or that of the Peixos [fish], from the Roman villa of Pineda. You could try and identify the close-on fifty marine animals that appear on it: octopuses, murenas, lobsters…

Also of interest is the popular bronze chandelier in the form of a young slave, known as the "El Negret" [The Young Black], from the 1st or 2nd century AD, and the collection of portraits and statues, with busts of emperors such as Hadrian, Marcus Aurelius or Trajan.

THE NECROPOLIS OF THE EARLY CHRISTIANS

In the Passeig de la Independència we will find, as occurred in the 1920s when they built a building close to the Tabacalera, one of the main necropolises of Europe, since during late antiquity Tarragona was still one of the main urban centres on the Peninsula. In a space of 20,000 square metres there are more than 2,000 tombs dating from the 3rd to the 6th century AD, with the remains of the city's first Christians. A unique item was found among these tombs, a 3rd century AD toy, a jointed marble doll that seems to be waiting for the little girl that played with it. We should also note the sarcophagi of the lions, the teacher and the apostles, and funerary mosaics.

In 1994 a Christian complex was located very nearby, inhabited from the 5th century AD, which can be visited in the basement of a shopping mall.

THE PROVINCIAL FORUM AND
A PRAETORIUM THAT NEVER WAS

The high part of the Roman city, above what is today the Rambla Vella, which separated it into two, was divided into three large terraces: in the upper terrace was the Religious Worship Area; in the central one the Representation Square, and in the lower one the Circus. The two highest ones formed the Provincial Forum, from where the Tarraco province was governed, even though this name is commonly given only to the Representation Square. This was a vast porticoed space measuring over seven hectares, built around 73 AD. In the chambers of the rectangular square, measuring 175 metres by more than 300 metres, the representatives of the provincial municipalities and colonies met, and the documents were archived in the *tabularium*. The current Forum square is less solemn, more popular and busier, with traditional bars and the local farmers' fruit and vegetable market that takes place every Saturday morning.

The Praetorium, the Castle of Pilate or the King has been given imaginative names, but not very rigorously, generally speaking. People saw the palace of a praetor or of the supposed Governor Pilate, Pontius Pilate –who was in fact governor of Judea– in what was a tower of stairs, although the building also housed administrative rooms. The name of Castell del Rei, king's castle, is more accurate, because here lived the monarchs when they came to Tarragona, both Jaume II and Pere III, who also both had it fitted out. In the walls of the Praetorium, which until 1950 was a prison, some cats who always seem to be there have established their dwelling place.

The Praetorium (Museum of the History of Tarragona) preserves the sarcophagus of Hippolytus, from the 3rd century AD. It was found in the sea in 1948, and explains the Greek myth of Phaedra and Hippolyte. The Tecleta, a female statue, also forms part of the MHT collections. People claimed it as their own and gave it the name of the saint when it was found in the City Park, although it is in fact a Roman sculpture.

THE BEST-PRESERVED CIRCUS IN EUROPE

The Circus was the most attended public spectacle of the Roman world, and the *aurigas*, or drivers of the chariots –*bigas*, with two horses, or *cuadrigas*, with four– were as popular then as the Formula 1 drivers of today. Two very well known *aurigas* were Fucus and Eutyches. Regarding the latter, in the Diocesan Museum there is a very poetical inscription that speaks of his illness and death while still in the prime of life. The Circus was built at the end of the 1st century AD and is over 300 metres long, more than twice that of a football pitch, and 100 metres wide. It housed a big crowd: 23,000 people. The head and part of the seating and vaults can be visited. The latter are very well preserved and were used as access or as changing rooms or shops.

Other vaults and remains of the Circus can be found in private houses, shops, bars or restaurants –one of them is called "Les Voltes"; a part of the platform is conserved in another, and a third, "El Cau", is one of the night spots that has live music. In the area around the head is the Muralleta, dating from 1363, and the Torre de les Monges or of Charles V, from the 14th century, reformed in the 16th century.

THE AMPHITHEATRE OF THE GLADIATORS AND THE MARTYRS

E ven today, in the 21st century, every year the Amphitheatre fills with gladiators and spectators who demand the sacrifice of the loser by pointing down to the ground, the kingdom of the dead –the gesture of the closed fist with the thumb pointing down is pure Hollywood fiction. Fortunately, these are historical reconstructions done by experts, as part of Tàrraco Viva. In the Amphitheatre, alongside the Miracle Park, measuring 130 metres by a little more than 100 metres, with terracing excavated out of some of the rock, and with a capacity in ancient times for 14,000 people, fights and hunting with wild animals also took place.

By 221 AD it already required reforms, an inscription has been found in it dedicated to the eccentric emperor Heliogabalus, who ordered its restoration, and which constitutes the biggest discovery to date regarding what was the Empire. In the same century, in 259, the first bishop of Tarragona, Saint Fructuosus, and the deacons Saint Augurius and Saint Eulogius, were burnt alive and martyred. A basilica was built in the arena in honour of the martyrs during the Visigoth period between the 6th and 7th centuries, and over that, in the 12-13th centuries, the Romanesque church of Santa Maria del Miracle.

Also in his memory, since 1990 The Passion of Saint Fructuosus has been performed. It is a theatrical work based on the Acts of Martyrdom of the bishop and deacons, the oldest preserved on the Peninsula, which provides us with an eyewitness account of the martyrdom and death of the saints: ancient and human heritage.

Santa Maria del Miracle
Abandoned by the sea
In the centre of the circle of waves
Of the gulls or the past.

Santa Maria del Miracle,
Waves and centuries come and go,
From Mallorca to Tarragona
And towards the voice from the blood.

Santa Maria del Miracle,
More majesty than loneliness.
The air slips over the cheeks
Of angels that were and will be.

They bring back centuries among the marbles.
The wood carries deep-rooted tradition in the air.
Santa Maria del Miracle.
Naked maidens and giants.

Oh seashell that echoes in the air,
Where the tide of the centuries flows
–Santa Maria del Miracle–
Towards the present from the past!

Refined and everlasting music
Running through the pebbles and the grass,
Santa Maria del Miracle,
Where Eternity anchored.

The air slips over the cheeks
Of angels that were and will be
Santa Maria del Miracle...

Murmur of prayers and horses.

Poem by Vicent Andrés Estellés
(The autumn in Tarragona is a *Tardor literària
amb els cinc sentits*, [Literary Autumn with the five
senses] with routes dedicated to writers who have
written about the city, among many other events).

THE FORUM OF THE COLONY, JUDICIAL AND ADMINISTRATIVE

I f the Provincial Forum was the space of the provincial administration, the Colony, Municipal or Low Forum was destined for the administration of the city and the judicial activity. Work began on it in the Republican period, although it was remodelled during the empire of Augustus Caesar, the "Tarraconense". It extended along what are currently the streets of Lleida, Cardenal Cervantes, Gasòmetre and Caputxins. Remains of a 2nd century temple, as well as a large juridical basilica have been discovered there.

THE DEVIL'S BRIDGE

There is no life or civilisation without water. The water for Tarraco came from two aqueducts, from the rivers Gaià and Francolí, though perhaps there was a third river as well. A section of the channel from the Francolí still survives, some five kilometres from the city, the Aqueduct of Les Ferreres. Its architecture is so solid that the post-Roman population thought that it could only be the work of the Devil, and that's where its popular name comes from. It was probably built in the 1st century AD, and is made up of a double row of arches, with 11 on the lower level and 25 on the upper level, 27 metres high and more than 200 metres long. It is located, moreover, within a beautiful setting of pine woods and undergrowth of bushes and grasses. The filmmaker Bigas Luna has given his own particular vision of it in the film *La teta i la lluna* [The tit and the moon], which describes other facets of the people from the Camp de Tarragona county.

THE MÈDOL, AND THE NEEDLE THAT STITCHED TARRACO TOGETHER

The Mèdol quarry is one of the most enigmatic spots of Tarragona. The centre is an enormous crater measuring 200 by 50 metres, the Clot del Mèdol. A stone obelisk, the *Agulla* [the Needle], some 16 metres high, points out the depth to which the material was extracted. With the passing of the centuries, in the Mèdol, which has been a setting for concerts –like those held in 1930– and inspiration to painters and writers, such as Josep Carner or Rovira i Virgili, a unique microclimate has been created of flora and fauna. A great many Roman buildings were constructed with its sandstone, easy to carve, and of a characteristic colour between yellow and gold, like honey.

CENTCELLES, VILLA AND MAUSOLEUM

To the south of Tarragona, in Constantí, is one of the most important funerary buildings in the country, the Christian Mausoleum of Centcelles, from the 4th century AD, with the oldest mosaics, of Christian subject matter, in the entire Roman world. In the large circular hall we can see hunting scenes, enthroned figures and representations of the seasons of the year and of the Old and New Testaments.

It had previously been a Roman villa, perhaps with one hundred rooms, *centum cellae*, from where the name of de Centcelles would have come, and had been occupied since the 2nd century BC.

LA VILLA DELS MUNTS

Six kilometres to the east, in the direction of Barcino, we find the previously mentioned Torre dels Escipions, a funerary monument that we do not know who it was built for. It has an almost square ground plan and must have had a triangular upper part.

Higher up, in the Altafulla district, on the hill known as Els Munts, there is a villa that is larger and richer than the majority of those known in other parts of Catalonia. This is due to the fact that it was the residence of an imperial official sent to Tarraco in the mid-2nd century AD, Caius Valerius Avitus. He was a duumvir, a type of magistrate, and he embellished an estate that was already in use in the first half of the 1st century AD. In the Villa dels Munts, which caught fire in the 3rd century AD, but which was still inhabited until perhaps the 7th century or early 8th century, luxury decorative elements have been found, such as paintings or statues, and the magnificent mosaics of the Muses −of the nine Muses, those of Thalia, Euterpe and Mnemosyne (the muses' mother) have been preserved−, which can be seen in the National Archaeological Museum.

In May, during the holding of Tarraco Viva, the owner of the house, Faustina, invites us to have some Roman aperitifs and to visit "her house", a dwelling with thermal baths, hot and cold swimming pools, a tepid water area, and another space for sweating.

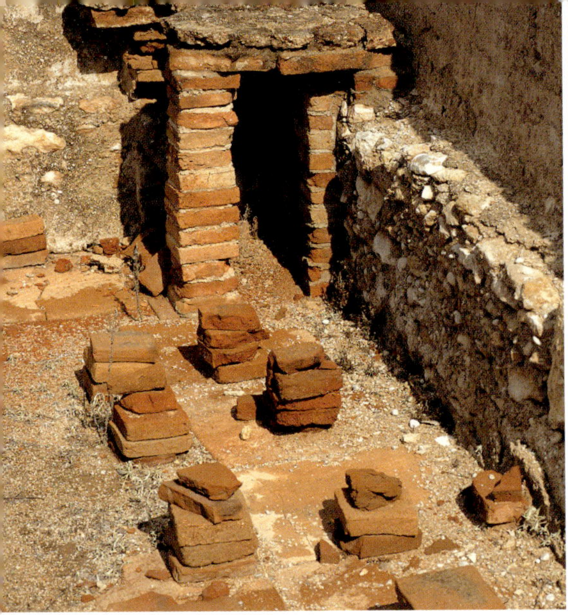
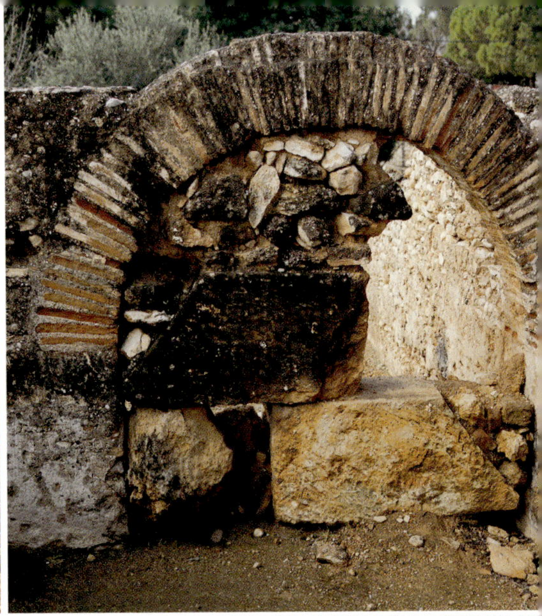
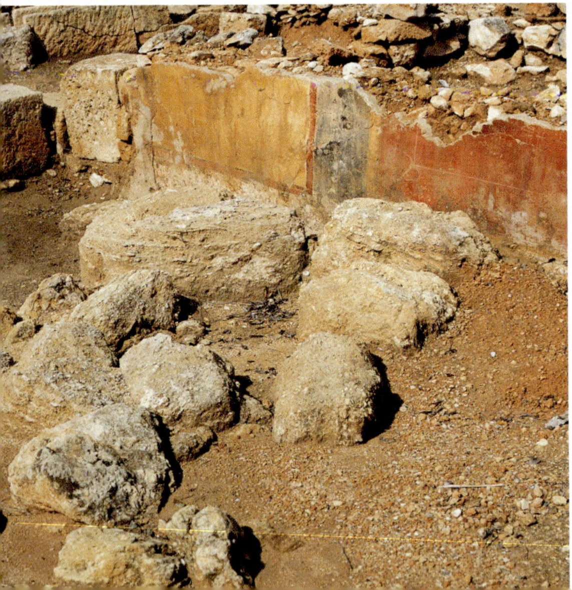
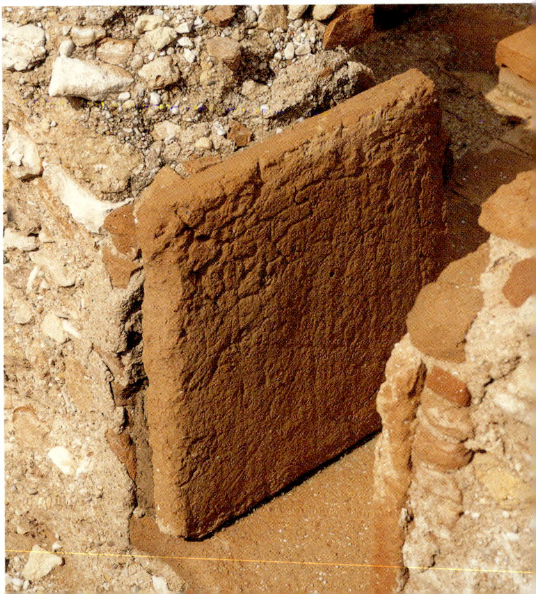

*Some fourteen Roman miles from
Tarragona, about twenty kilometres
–each Roman mile, or one thousand
steps, are 1,482 metres–, in Roda, is the*
ARC DE BERÀ. *The arch, so symbolic
and so much reproduced on all kinds
of objects, is the most important of
those known in the old* Provincia
Tarraconensis, *and it was found right
on the Via Augusta, the Roman way.
Not that many years ago, the main
road still passed beneath it. It was
probably built in the times of Augustus.*

MEDIEVAL TARRAGONA
AND THE PART ALTA

VISIGOTH METROPOLIS

In the 4th century AD, the Tarragona province was occupied by the Visigoths. Until the 8th century, Tarragona was an ecclesiastical metropolis and continued being the capital of the province. There are no monuments remaining from that period, because the Visigoths preferred to adapt Roman buildings. To start with the occupiers believed in Arianism, whereas the Hispano-Roman peoples were Catholics. The Catholic bishop maintained the status of the city under Visigoth domination and later, in the attempts to revive the church during the Muslim occupation.

In the moments prior to the fall of the Visigoth monarchy, Tarracona –this was the form it appeared in the 6th century in Vulgar Latin– formed part of the independent kingdom made up of Catalonia and Septimania. The Muslim Al-Hurr occupied part of these territories and must have laid siege on Tarragona in 716. The metropolitan bishop fled to Liguria with the relics of the saints Fructuosus, Augurius and Eulogius. The city was not left completely depopulated, but by the 11th century it had become no-man's land, between Christians and Muslims. A 15th-century author, Al-Himrayi, describes the city of Tarakuna in a dream-like way, basing himself on two writers, also Muslims, from the 11-12th centuries, in a text included by Josep Maria Recassens in his *Història de Tarragona*:

"Its ancient monuments remain in place without having suffered any damage. Most of its walls survive without having collapsed. It is the city where there is more carved marble. Its walls are of black and white marble, and it is difficult to come across others in any way similar. One of the curiosities of Tarragona is the mills built by the ancient inhabitants, which turn when the wind blows and stop when it is still. The people versed in the Latin language say that Tarragona means land similar to a dwelling place of demons".

CHRISTIAN REPOPULATION

It was not demons, however, that came to Tarragona to make it their dwelling place. In 1091, Pope Urban II re-established the metropolitan see of the city. In the early 11th century, a small number of Christians started to repopulate the territory. The formal restoration, nevertheless, took place with the involvement of the Norman knight Robert Bordet, or Aguiló, to whom the Bishop of Barcelona, Oleguer, gave the city as a fiefdom and awarded him the title of Prince of Tarragona in 1129.

Tarragona's medieval age of splendour was the second half of the 13th century and the 14th century. In 1228, King Jaume I announced to the city, during a stay in the house of the merchant Pere Martell, his intention of conquering Mallorca. The Black Death wreaked havoc on the city in the 14th and 15th centuries. In 1462, in the civil war between the Generalitat and Joan II, during which Tarragona sided with the former, there was a siege. The harvest was lost, there was a decrease in population and economic bankruptcy hit the city.

The medieval city within the walls is known as Part Alta [high part]. It has been substantially rehabilitated in recent years, with warm-coloured façades.

THE PLAÇA DEL PALLOL

Immediately after passing through the Portal del Roser, the Plaça del Pallol represents a long trip back in time, to the medieval city. The name comes from that of the warehouse where the city's wheat was stored in the Middle Ages, and for which the official, the *palloler*, was responsible. The square stands over the old Provincial Forum. The Voltes del Pallol are precisely this, some vaults of the Forum. Facing us is a wall, and an arch that leads to the Forum itself.

In the nearby Old Courthouse, a neo-classical building that occupies an ancient entry tower between the Circus and the Forum, we come across a painting that nobody has any intention of wiping away: it is the only one preserved in Tarragona of the Civil War.

Little remains of the Call [Jewish quarter], apart from the historical memory and the Gothic arches in Carrer de Talavera. **THE JEWISH QUARTER** spread around the Plaça dels Àngels, which until the 18th century was still called Plaça del Call. It was made up of five narrow streets, and had a synagogue, school, baths and a narrow doorway that led to the outside.

▶

In the cloister of the Pontifical Seminary, a building from the late 19th century, **THE CHAPEL OF SANT PAU** is hidden, from the mid-13th century, situated on a rock from where the saint would have preached during his hypothetical stay in 63 AD. The truth is that he expressed in writing his intention of coming, but it is not certain whether in fact he did. Near to here is the church of Santa Tecla la Vella and, in Carrer de les Coques, the old Hospital de Santa Tecla, now the Tarragona County Council building.

THE GOTHIC MARKET IN CARRER MERCERIA

If you stroll around Carrer Mercería on a Sunday morning, you will come across, just like in the nearby Pla de la Seu, a little antique market, or of old things, whichever way you like, with postcards, books, fossils… It is a labyrinth of a thousand objects and a thousand stories in the space of a few metres. In the 14th century, in the Gothic arcades of Carrer Merceria there had also been a market, but of vegetables. Change old records for cabbages, then –that's where the name of the adjoining square comes from–, in order to get closer still to those times of yesteryear.

The **CARRER DE CAVALLERS** is a cobbled, shady and cool street. It is usually a calm redoubt, even when the rest of the Part Alta crackles with fireworks and festivities. This is where the lords lived, the Cavallers, despite the lack of a extensive nobility in the city during the Middle Ages, due to the fact that it was a fief of the Church. In any case, the name does not date back before the 15th century. It is one of the streets that conserve its old aspect the best. The marquises of Montoliu lived here until 1880, and the lords of Castellarnau, who left behind two of the most important palaces. Casa Montoliu houses the Music Conservatory, while we will deal with Casa Castellarnau as a museum.

▶

The **CARRER MAJOR** [main street] arose as such during the Middle Ages. Today it is a central and crowded street, with antique and select food and drink shops, which preserves examples of civil architecture such as the Casa de la Generalitat, the Old City Hall or the Casa de l'Abat de Poblet, on the corner of Carrer de l'Abat.

THE FLIGHT OF STEPS AND THE PLA DE
LA SEU, THE STREET THEATRE

The flight of steps that leads from Carrer Major to the Cathedral is the terracing from where you can sit watching the great annual spectacles that are held in the streets of the Part Alta. On these occasions the steps, bordered by the fountains in the Plaça de les Cols, fills with spectators who are, at the same time, the actors.

In the Pla de la Seu, or the Cathedral, the medieval acropolis, there are stately buildings that belonged to families of the aristocracy or clerics. One of them is the old Palau de la Cambreria [chamberlain], with a façade of Gothic and Renaissance windows. It lost its status when the Papacy removed the rank of Chamberlain –who provided the clergy with their clothing– in the 15th century. It housed the monarchs when they came to the city, and was later known as Casa Balcells. Beside it, we can see one of the more curious and oldest houses, the Casa dels Porxos.

THE CATEDRAL

THE CATEDRAL, THE ART OF THE CENTURIES

The Cathedral is imposing. The façade of the Final Judgement, from the 15th century, with Christ judging mankind, surrounded by prophets and apostles, is the visible part of the Romanesque and Gothic, and Renaissance and Baroque ensemble, the fullest and richest of the city: an artistic ensemble that we will discover fully inside, in the Cloister and in the Diocesan Museum.

The metropolitan see and primate occupies what we might call a hill of divinity, with historical and religious continuity since the Roman period. It is raised over a Roman centre of worship, which successively became a Romano-Christian basilica, a Visigoth church and a 12th century Romanesque temple, before this highly important transitional construction from Romanesque to Gothic. Work began on it in 1171, and in the mid-14th century, the Black Death and the subsequent lack of workforce and money meant that it remained unfinished.

The sides, with a large gateway, are Romanesque, and in the wall we can find earlier elements, such as a 4th century Christian sarcophagus. The Virgin and Child stand out over the mullion, the central column of the Gothic gateway. Like a giant eye observing the misdemeanours we get up to in the adjoining streets, an enormous Gothic rose window overlooks everything.

THE GOTHIC ALTARPIECE OF SAINT THEKLA

L et's go inside the Cathedral, a Latin cross church with three naves and a transept. Perhaps the best time to do so, because of the light, is between 10 and 11 in the morning in summer or autumn and early afternoon, around 3 o'clock, in the spring. The apse is Romanesque, as is the front part of the high altar. This front is made of marble and shows scenes from the life and martyrdom of the protomartyr Thekla. Around it we can observe impressive Romanesque flooring.

The altarpiece is also dedicated to the patron saint, and is one of the most important in the country, the work of Pere Joan, from the first third of the 15th century. The altarpiece ensemble is dominated by an alabaster figure of the Virgin with Child, with figures of Saint Thekla and Saint Paul at the side. It is a composition full of life and of tiny details, such as the realist faces of all the people that appear in it, each one given an individual expression and personality.

THE SEPULCHRE OF ARCHBISHOP JOAN D'ARAGÓ AND THE GOTHIC CHAPELS

O n the side wall of the presbytery is the tomb of Archbishop Joan d'Aragó, son of King Jaume II. Over the sarcophagus, in 1337 an anonymous sculptor completed the reclining figure of the patriarch of Alexandria, with a smile on their face.

The oldest chapel is that of Saint Ollegarius, from the 12th century, and the chapels of the Virgin of the Tailors, Saint Lucy, the Corpus Christi, Saint Michael and the Eleven Thousand Virgins are all Gothic constructions.

THE GOTHIC CHOIR AND THE 16TH CENTURY ORGAN

T he carefully worked wooden seating of the choir dates from 1479. It was commissioned to be built by Archbishop Pedro de Urrea, who captained the ships that Pope Calixtus III sent to fight against the Turks. His banner, with the keys of Saint Peter, hangs from the central nave of the Cathedral. From the 16th century it became the housing for the main organ, one of the largest in Europe. It was designed by Jaume Amigó, a priest from Tivissa who became an architect while living in Rome.

ONE OF THE OLDEST BELLS IN EUROPE

The bell tower has a Romanesque base, but the other two sections are Gothic. The upper section contains fifteen bells. Some of these bells are the oldest still in use in Europe: the bell named Assumpta dates from 1313; and Fructuosa, from 1314, the pealing of both being so essential in the annual festival of Saint Thekla. Others, such as the famous Capona, the hour bell, were added in 1509, or in the 18th and 19th centuries, and have names such as Tecla, Sorda, Vedada or Maria Bàrbara.

THE CLOISTER, A BOOK OF STONE

The cloister is almost square, about 45 metres on the side. It is quiet and austere, of a more monastic peace than urban, with iron grilles that were fitted in the 16th century to protect the garden, then a conventual orchard. It was begun in the 12th century and crowned with a Gothic vault. The capitals are Romanesque and with a great iconographic diversity, veritable pages of "stone" for "readers" who did not know how to read. They represent scenes from the bible, minstrels, monstrous beasts and even the months of the year.

Some serve to tell a moral tale, such as the very well known cyma with the procession of rats, which demonstrates that cunning prevails over force, and does so by recounting how a cat that wants to catch rats plays dead, and when the rats pick him up to bury him, he "resuscitates" in order to catch them. There are other curious capitals, such as the one about the fox, similar to the previous one, or the one about the three faces, in reality just one, that shows three completely different expressions, according the spot you look at it from.

On the floor you can see two boards set in, like chessboards, which were used for the games of the altar boys. In the cloister is the chapel of the Virgin of the same name (16th century), one of the most popular Tarragona devotions, with a 13th-century carving.

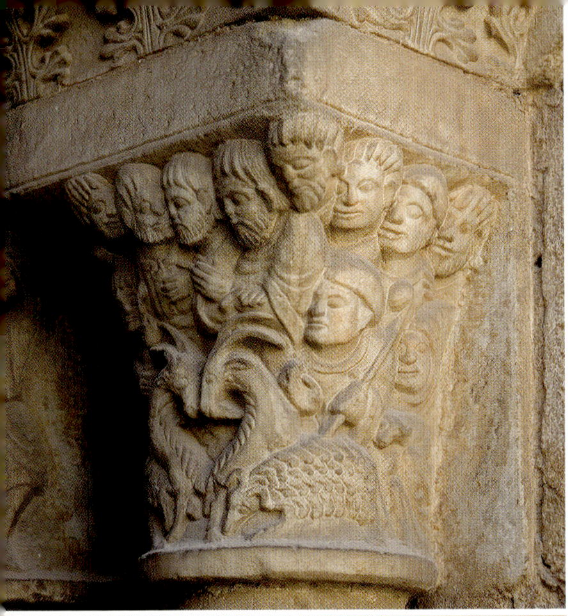
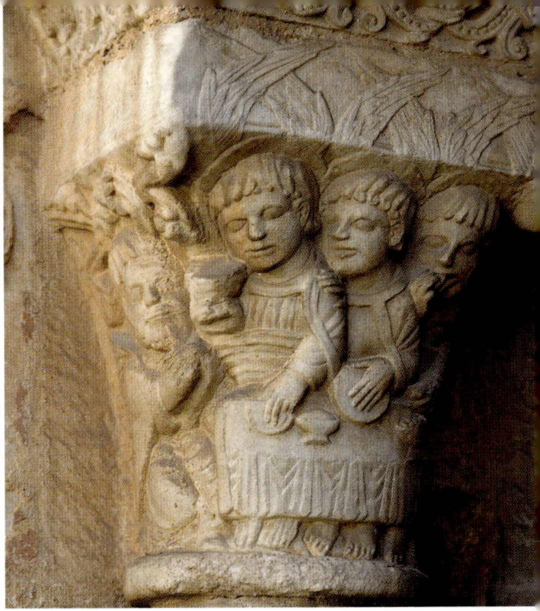
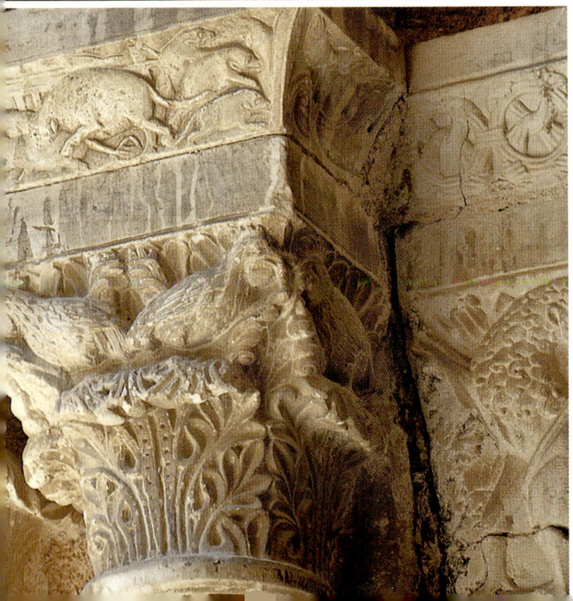
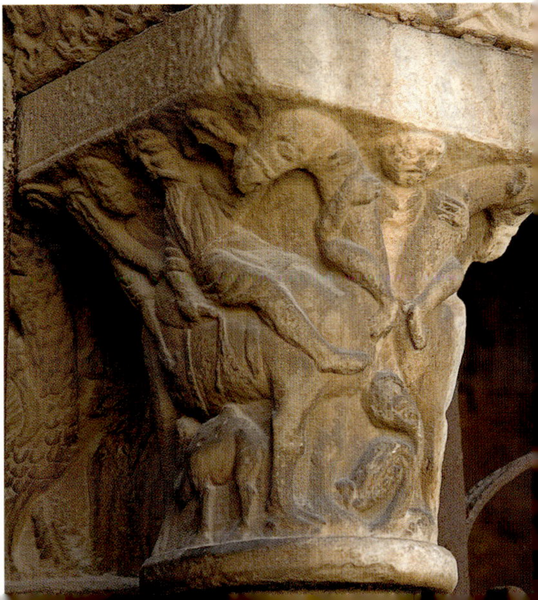

THE ROMANESQUE PORTAL *between the Cloister and the Cathedral, from the first half of the 13th century, sculpted in white marble, is quite magnificent and has a Christ on the tympanum surrounded by the symbols of the four evangelists, and on the capitals, the birth of Jesus and another very odd scene representing an angel awakening the Three Kings of the Orient, who are sleeping together, so that they can escape from Herod.*

We have already mentioned that the Cathedral guards more artistic treasures in its **DIOCESAN MUSEUM**. *Access is from the Cloister and it houses important collections. From Roman archaeology we would point out the funerary stele of the* auriga *Eutyches –do you remember him?: the hero of the Circus– or the sarcophagus of Apollo and the nine Muses. From the Hispano-Arab era, there is an Islamic large window dating from 960, and from the Gothic, the collection of paintings, altarpieces and panels, with the small board of the Annunciation, attributed to Jaume Huguet, the great 15th-century painter from Valls, or the altarpiece of Saint Michael, attributed to Bernat Martorell. The Museum contains Renaissance and Baroque items, such as the astonishing carving of Saint Christ, which can be seen in the Sacristy, and an important set of tapestries, such as the Tapestry of the Good life, from the 15th century, probably produced in Arras, France, and which gives us an almost complete view of life, the arts, customs and sciences of that century. The Treasure Room also features a 14th-century Gothic Mudejar coffered ceiling.*

THE 16TH TO 18TH CENTURIES

THREE CENTURIES AND TWO WARS

The city was strengthened from the 16th century, until during the Reaper's War, as from 1640, it became a fortified town and was under siege on two occasions. It was the first armed conflict to impede the city's growth during the modern era. Moreover, in the 16th and 18th centuries epidemics and pirate attacks were continuous, and towers and bastions were built as defence against the latter, such as the Torre de la Móra, in 1562, or the Tamarit bastion, in 1617.

For all these reasons the economy of the Camp de Tarragona region went into crisis, and was unable to recover until the 18th century, with the reconstruction of the port and the establishment of free trade with America. Not everything was negative, however. The humanist archbishops who lived in the 16th century, Gaspar Cervantes de Gaeta (1568-1575) –who has the Carrer Cardenal Cervantes named alter him– and Antoni Agustí (1577-1586), created the University and turned the city into a cultural centre.

The second conflict was the War of Succession, at the beginning of the 18th century. Tarragona was defended by a British garrison, which built the Falsa Braga and forts such as those of La Reina and Sant Jordi, both of them in the Punta del Miracle.

Other examples from this period are the Portal de Sant Antoni, built in the first half of the 18th century, and the Cross of the same name, built in 1604, or the Palau de la Diputació, County Hall, the old Charity house, from the late 17th century.

MODERNIST TARRAGONA AND THE 19th TO 21st CENTURIES

FROM A THIRD WAR TO THE NEW DISTRICTS IN THE 20TH CENTURY

The 19th century began with another war, the "French" war, with devastating consequences for Tarragona. On the 28th of June 1811, the attack by the Napoleonic army after a siege resulted in two years of misery, hunger and practically the total destruction of the city. Napoleon had defined himself as the Attila of Venice. Marhall Suchet was the Attila of Tarragona.

Economic recovery was slow, but boosted by the appearance of a commercial petit bourgeoisie. The Sant Joan wall began to be demolished and new streets linked the Part Alta and the newly built coastal district.

Chemical industries were established in the city in the mid-20th century, and around 1975, the refinery, with its night-time appearance of lights and flames, futurist and unreal. Immigration increased the population and the outlying districts grew in size, such as Bonavista, Torreforta –named alter a fortified mansion–, Campclar, Icomar, Riuclar, Sant Salvador, and Sant Pere i Sant Pau, an area that has around 25,000 inhabitants. These districts have developed their own personalities, centralities and attractions. Every Sunday Bonavista hosts a busy street market where you can find just about everything.

Of the architecture from the second half of the 20th century the Government Sub-delegation building is of note, a rationalist work by Alejandro de la Sota, as is the Universitat Laboral, the Ciutat Residencial or the Col·legi d'Arquitectes, by Rafael Moneo.

The **PALAU MUNICIPAL** is
not only the City Hall. It is
also the luxurious backdrop
to many festivals, the focal
point of those watching the
Diables, the Castells or the
Balls, which are the firework
parades, human towers and
dances. In the Middle Ages
it had been a Franciscan
convent and until the confis-
cation of church properties in
1835 was the convent of Sant
Domènec. After exclaustra-
tion it was used as a City
and Provincial Hall. In
the 1860s the neo-classical
façade was completed, with
effigies of important figures
from the history of the city.
Also of note is the stairway.

King Jaume I is buried in the monastery of Poblet, where his remains were moved from the Cathedral. The move, ordered by Franco in 1952, was not well received by the city. In the courtyard of the City hall is what should have been the **MAUSOLEUM OF KING JAUME I** in the Cathedral, planned by one of the great architects of Modernism, Lluís Domènec i Muntaner. It was kept in storage until 1992 when it was placed here.

THE PLAÇA DE LA FONT WAS THE CIRCUS ARENA

The Circus, which separated the official city from the inhabited one, reached as far as what are today Carrer Ferrers and Carrer Enrajolat, and to the Rambla Vella, on the long sides, and Carrer Salines and Passeig de Sant Antoni on the short sides. If you want to relive the crowded atmosphere of a day at the Circus, then go the Plaça de la Font on Sunday at aperitif time, just before lunch, or any day of the year if the weather is good enough to be out on the street. The emblematic square –just like in Rome's Piazza Navona, built over the stadium of Domiciano– occupies part of the Circus arena.

The Plaça de la Font is the agora that shows us the rhythms of changes that have taken place over the centuries. In the 13th century it became the Corral, an open-air space, an inhabited poor district, where in the 14th century fairs were held. During the 16th century it had a public fountain, which would eventually give it its name, despite the fact that it was not called this until the 18th century.

CASA CASTELLARNAU, *in Carrer Cavallers, is the home of the Museum of the History of Tarragona, which also manages the Roman monuments, amongst them the Praetorium. In Casa Castellarnau we can see Roman walls, but the vaulting of the ground floor is the constructive origins of the house, in the 14th and 15th centuries. The façade dates from the 18th century, when a new layout for it was undertaken. Emperor Charles v did not therefore find it as it is today when he passed through the city in 1542 and slept in the house. Neither was it called Castellarnau in those days, since this influential family bought it in the 18th century. The house possesses Baroque furnishings and objects, and a neo-classical room, with fresco paintings by Josep Flaugier, from the late-18th century.*

METROPOL THEATRE, JUJOL'S FIRST WORK

Josep Maria Jujol, who was born in Tarragona in 1879, is one of the great Catalan architects of all times, a man ahead of his time, both aesthetically and technically. Despite having worked with Gaudí, he had his own recognisable language. The Metropol Theatre, restored by Josep Llinàs in 1995, is one of the most outstanding works that he left to his city and his very first individual professional commission. It is a maritime allegory, with his illustrations of waves and fish, and the forms of keel and boat, but it is also full of religious symbolism, such as the m's of the Virgin Mary, of whom Jujol was a devout follower.

THE SGRAFFITO DESIGNS AND
BENCHES OF THE CASA XIMENIS

In 1914 Jujol received the commission to construct a building attached to La Muralla, and as a response to the difficulty of the task not only produced a house that respected history, but also a filigree of sgraffitos and iron. He made balconies and benches in this material that were very true to his own style, benches where people could sit and watch, chat or where fiancés could talk sweet nothings with each other. Casa Ximenis, as central as it is discrete, is highlighted by the thousands of lights that fall on the façade throughout the year.

Jujol is the author in his city, among other works, of the lady chapel of the Convent of the Carmelites, a building with an outstanding silhouette, known as La Punxa, built in 1918. As well as for its form, the convent is popular because the Agua del Carmen was manufactured here, a remedy for all ills that would be in every home.

A CENTRAL VIENNESE MARKET

In Plaça Corsini is one of the most-visited spots in the city each day, the Central market, heir in some ways to the Municipal Forum, with the stands of fish, vegetables and meat... It was built in 1915 by an architect with many buildings in the city, Josep Maria Pujol de Barberà. It is a large and elegant building, recalling the metro station of Karlplatz, in Vienna, by the architect Otto Wagner. On Tuesdays and Thursdays there is a traditional and popular street market selling clothes and other items.

Other interesting examples of Modernism in Tarragona are the Theresan College, the old Abbatoir, now the rectory building of the Rovira i Virgili University, Casa Salas, the Quinta de Sant Rafael, located in the Parc de la Ciutat, and the Casa de la Punxa –not to be confused with the Carmelite building–, currently the offices of the Chamber of Commerce.

THE RAMBLA IS ALWAYS NEW

The Rambla Nova is a wide passage, forty-five metres, and bright, a huge open-air hall, which at the beginning of the 21st century celebrates its 150th anniversary. In 1854 the first stone of the Sant Joan wall (16th century) was knocked down, and in 1859 the first house was built there.

It still spreads towards the River Francolí, and is the setting for all kinds of events, from processions to dances and fairs. Going from one end to another we come across monuments and sculptures. One is of a likable character, grandfather Virgili, a diarist who, seated on a bench and leaning on his stick, watches us as we pass by.

The Centenary Fountain is also here, commemorating one hundred years of the Rambla Nova, as is the monument in honour of the castellers, *the human towers –a* quatre de vuit *(a formation of tower) by the sculptor Francesc Anglès, unveiled in 1999– and the symbolic statue of the* Despullats *[Undressed]. It is a work by the great sculptor from Móra d'Ebre, Julio Antonio, who pays homage to the resisters of the 1811 siege. Due to the scandal raised by the nudes it was not put in place until 1931, 12 years after the sculptor had died.*

In 1960, the Tarragona writer Josep Anton Baixeras said of this sculptural group, in a local radio programme he regularly appeared in called Full de calendari: "Our city possesses an important privilege: it is sculpturally represented by the female figure of the group; in other words, Tarragona possesses a figurative interpretation, of high artistic value, which does not occur in too many cities in the world". *Speaking about the author, he ended by saying,* "the Tarragona that he chiselled out is the best Tarragona, the Tarragona that we would like to be eternal".

ADMIRAL ROGER DE LLÚRIA

T he statue of Admiral Roger de Llúria was unveiled in 1889. It came from Italy, like the admiral himself, where it had been created by the sculptor Fèlix Ferrer, son of Móra d'Ebre –the capital of the Ribera d'Ebre county has provided two works for the Rambla– and settled in Rome. Back to the sea and facing the city, he sits over a base by the architect Ramon Salas, also the author of the Balcony.

TOUCHING IRON ON THE MEDITERRANEAN BALCONY

Like a geometric tattoo drawn on a visible part of the body, the Mediterranean Balcony is Tarragona's emblematic trademark, something that makes it unmistakable. From an everyday point of view, it is a ritual destination, which means that strolling down the Rambla and reaching the railings is a ritual that, more than a superstition, is a form of identity. The President of the First Spanish Republic, Emilio Castelar, was the person who gave it the name of the Mediterranean Balcony. In the empty space facing the Balcony of over 40 metres in height there was once a quarry, from which the rock was extracted to build the port.

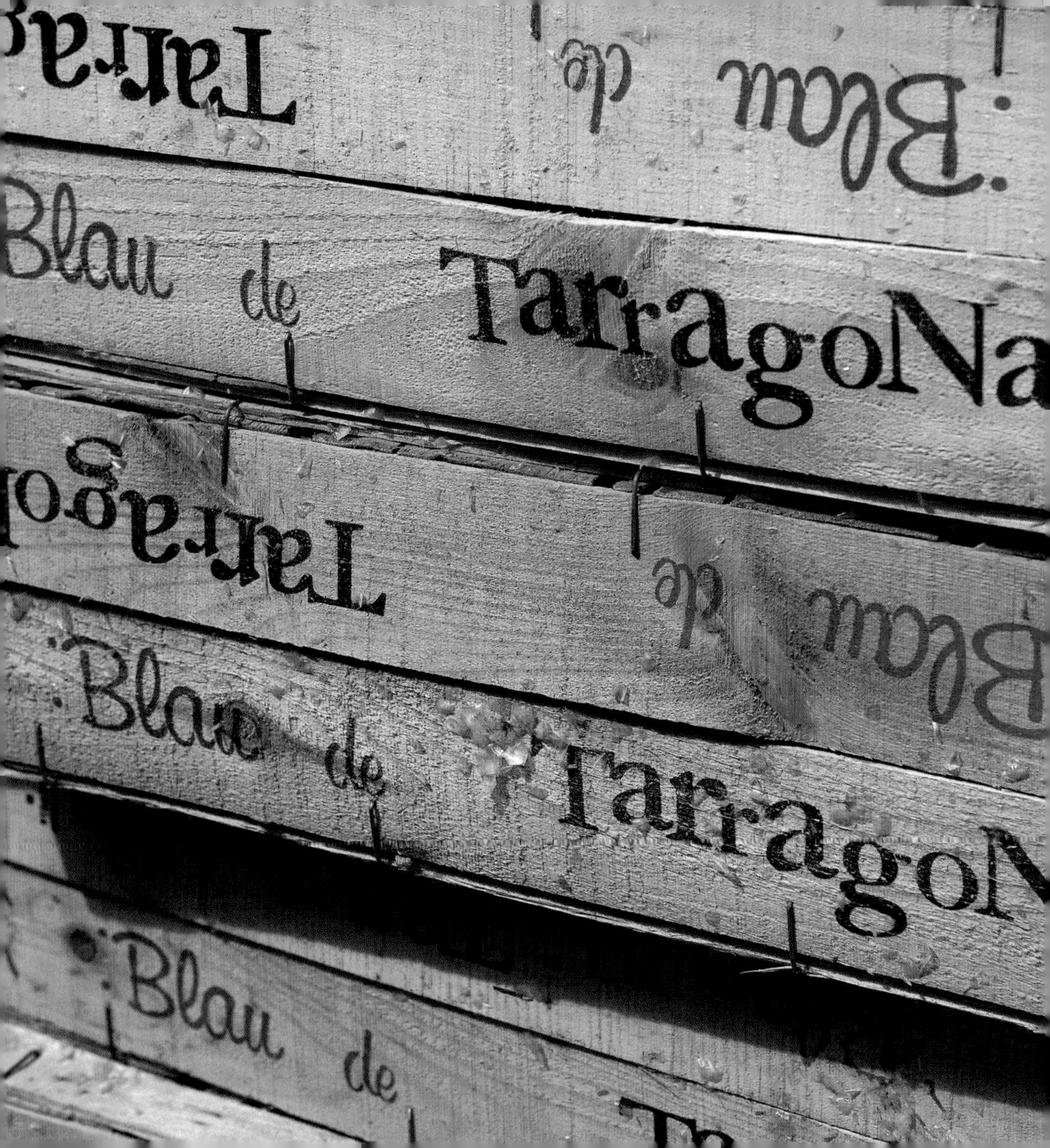
Blau de TarragoNa
Blau de Tarrago
Blau de TarragoN
Blau de

EL SERRALLO
AND THE PORT

EL SERRALLO, THE CITY OF THE SEA

El Serrallo is Tarragona, but it is another Tarragona. The seaside district is that of the fishermen, the fish restaurants −ask the people from here which one they would recommend−, of the stands, also of fish, which fill up when the hot weather arrives, with women sewing nets, and of the arrival of the boats, or "pes", which is what the locals of El Serrallo call the fish market. It is also a district that is changing, due to the disappearance of the barriers that separated it from the city. The district, situated between the River Francolí, the port and the railway line, arose in the second half of the 19th century, when the construction of the track meant that the fishermen's houses had to be moved there.

ROMAN PORT AND LEISURE JETTY

The port, as we have mentioned above, when we talked about the Roman times, began to be built then, and has been modernised and enlarged throughout history: in the 13th and 15th centuries, and as from 1790 −with stones transported by prisoners−... Since its origins, just as today, it has been one of the key trading ports in the Mediterranean.

The fishing port, opened in 1942, is the number one port in Catalonia for trawling and line fishing. The sea around Tarragona is good for catching hake, sea bass, dorado and swordfish... It has a very wide coastal platform, the "sec", aided by the sediments left by the River Ebre.

The Nautical Club has its centre in the sports port, which has been around for over 125 years, and in recent times a night spot area has developed, with restaurants and bars.

THE CHURCH OF SANT PERE

In the centre of El Serrallo is Sant Pere. It is obviously the local saint's day festival, held on the 29th of June, but we refer now to the parish church. The neo-Gothic single-nave building is the work of Ramon Salas i Ricomà, and is the most characteristic of El Serrallo. Archbishop Constantí Bonet, defender of papal infallibility, had it built in 1878.

In the eastern dock is one of the first buildings that can be seen on reaching Tarragona from the sea –an arrival that gives you an incredible view of the city–, the **PORT CLOCK**. It is in the form of a shrine, with tour Ionic columns, and was designed by the port manager in 1922. Despite its poetic appearance, its objective is prosaic: to tell the port workers the time.

The **WAREHOUSES** and old refuges are currently used for different activities, ranking from exhibitions to fairs. They were built in the early 20th century and measure around 60 x 15 metres.

►

THE PLAÇA DELS CARROS is the centre of what is now called the Port district, the heart of the marine that connects with the Part Alta along Carrer de la Unió. This district has two main ways, Carrer Apodaca and Carrer Reial. The port workers and the goods warehouse workers were hired in the square, which owes its name to the port transport [carro, cart]. Until the last century, that is the 20th century, the district was full of wine cellars, and was a spot with the atmosphere of a working port and traditional life.

A LIGHTHOUSE OF THE EBRE IN THE PORT OF TARRAGONA?

The old lighthouse at the Banya point, which from 1864 was on the coastline of the Delta de l'Ebre, was placed in the Tarragona port in 1986. Now restored, it is a perfect spot to watch the sea, the arrival of the boats, or to drink vermouth –Izaguirre, the locally produced drink, with cellars in Morell– or eat in the restaurant there.

BEACHES, GREEN SPACES AND TOWNS IN THE AREA

Tarragona is a large municipal area, with many kilometres of beaches, with woods and unspoilt areas, some of them officially protected, and a small constellation of towns and villages each with their own character. One of then, Canonja, a town with a very active community life, which was annexed by Tarragona in 1964, has been taking the first steps to become an independent town again.

SPORTS, CITY AND SOUTH SEA BEACHES

Without having to go very far, by city transport or on foot, Tarragona has all kinds of beaches imaginable. Some of them are large and with sports areas, such as La Llarga or l'Arrabassada. There are other city beaches, a stone's throw from home, such as La Comandància or El Miracle. There are popular, but not too crowded, beaches such as La Savinosa, Els Capellans, or those of Tamarit and La Móra.

There are also secluded beaches, such as Els Cossis, beside the Punta del Miracle, and heavenly beaches, and nudist beaches. Close to the Escipiones, in the protected area of the Bosc de la Marquesa, going along a few paths that run through pine woods, we reach the beaches of Calabecs (or Roca Plana, or l'Arboçar: they have lots of names) and Cala Fonda, more commonly known by the name, with Hawaiian echoes, as Waikiki.

A BRITISH CEMETERY IN LA PUNTA DEL MIRACLE

On the road that runs along the coast there is one of the city's most unusual spots. The closed iron gate of the English Cemetery hides from curiosity a place —more befitting the Cornish coast, for example— where non-catholic sailors and other persons from foreign boats were buried. It is British territory and is also known as the Cemetery of the English. The Tarragona writer Olga Xirinacs describes it to us in the novel *Zona marítima*: *"In that crypt had been the oldest tombs in the graveyard. It was built in eighteen forty four, but housed the remains that had been buried in Camp de Mart. They were those of the British soldiers who had fought in the War of Succession".*

THE OLD TOWN OF TAMARIT

Until the 1950s, Tamarit de Mar was a district that included the 11th-century castle and the Romanesque church, and the town of Ferran, the capital of the district, and that of Monnars or Molnàs. In 1055, the Count of Barcelona Ramon Berenguer I granted the castle and title of Viscount of Tarragona to Bernat Amat de Claramunt, with the intention of conquering the city. At the beginning of the 20th century, the North American patron Charles Deering bought and reformed the castle.

THE HERMITAGES

If you want to know where the Loreto hermitage is, ask us where the Llorito, the little parrot, is. The sanctuary, leaving the city in an eastwards direction, was built in 1957, and replaced another one that had been destroyed in 1823. It had originally been built to house a figure brought from Italy by a priest in the 16th century. This priest had been to visit Archbishop Doria, primate of Tarragona, who never set foot in this city. Another hermitage is that of La Salut, by the architect Salas i Ricomà.

A CAVE BENEATH OUR FEET

It is not outside the city, but beneath it. A large cave was discovered in 1996 beneath Carrer Gasòmetre, which occupies a large area of the low part of the city. It contains a Roman gallery, from the period in which its water was used.

A YEAR IN TARRAGONA: FESTIVALS AND TRADITIONS

CRAFT CARNIVAL

With a very high level of participation, over 3,000 people dressed in hand-crafted costumes. This is how Carnival is celebrated in Tarragona, which has authentic elements such as the Bóta de Carnaval, a huge barrel, painted by local artists, that recalls medieval wine distribution. It is placed in the Plaça de la Font and is burnt on Ash Tuesday, the day —and not Wednesday— that the *Carnestoltes* [the Carnaval King] is buried in Tarragona.

The celebration begins on the Sunday before Carnival week with the popular *Xarró* stew. On the Saturday of Carnival the grand parade takes place, the Rua de la Artesania, the best attended event, and on the Sunday, the Rua de Lluïment [Sparkle] and the Flight of Doctor Mistela, a character who with this drink tries to bring *Carnestoltes* back to life, and everyone else come to that, after the ravages of the festival. The king is accompanied to the burial by the Concubine and he is burnt in it in the form of *Ninot* and *Ninota*, two satirical figures that are heirs of Roman festivals such as Lupercal and Saturnal.

THE DEVILS SPEAK AND THROW FIRE

In the burning of the barrel and the dolls, as in the Saturday parade, with the animals of fire of the *Seguici Popular de Tarragona* [Funeral cortege], the Dragon, Ox and *Víbria*, another mythical dragon, there is the *Ball de Diables* [Devil's Dance] firework dance, which occurs on several occasions throughout the year, such as in the festival of Saint Thekla. It is a spoken dance, an example of popular theatre in the Camp de Tarragona and Penedès counties, of a distant origin, documented regularly as from the Middle Ages and recovered in 1984. Tarragona, therefore, is a land of devils. Perhaps the Arab Himrayi was right after all.

On Saint Thekla's Day the *Ball de Sant Miquel* and *Diables* is held, which reporesents the struggle between Good and Evil, and where the *Versots* are read out, verses that sum up the year in satirical rhymes, critical of the local politicians, above all. Every devil carries a mace from which they launch fireworks, such as Catherine wheels or fountains. They are led by Lucifer and the she-devil, a role played by a man.

THE EASTER MYSTERIES

For anyone who has not been in Tarragona on Good Friday, or any other day during Holy Week, coming during the procession of the Sant Enterrament could be an unexpected experience. It is surprising to see, in a city that at other times is noisy and irreverent, more than 5,000 dressed in tunics carrying, in many cases on their shoulders, as many as twenty processional floats.

It is even more surprising to discover the procession of the Sant Enterrament, the most typical in Catalonia, a traditional festival of national interest, and one of the most impressive in the whole State, has continued, with a few exceptions that can be counted on one hand, since the mid-16th century, organised by the Royal and Venerable Congregation of the Pure Blood of Our Lord Jesus Christ, which today participates in it alongside another ten brotherhoods.

Apart from the other events held in Holy Week, such as the *Via Crucis*, the Way of the Cross, Good Friday begins in the afternoon with the collection of the floats by the *Armats*, the Roman soldiers, in the Rambla Nova and the streets of the Part Alta as far as the church of Nazaret in the Plaça del Rei. A tense moment during the procession is the raising of the mysteries up the steep Baixada de la Peixateria. A notable float is that of Saint Sepulchre, of the Farmers' Guild, with a 17th-century Baroque image, the oldest preserved, with the sepulchre designed by Josep Maria Jujol, who also designed The Pietà, of the same Guild. The only mystery preserved whole from before the Civil War is The Cyrene, from 1930, owned by the Brotherhood of Jesus of Nazareth, which saved part of their float, The Nazarene (1907).

TÀRRACO, VIVA

Every May, the Roman Tarraco comes back to life, and the city is filled with togas and robes. They are the days of the historical conferences called Tarraco Viva, organised by the Museum of the History of Tarragona, which take place in the Camp de Mart and in the Roman buildings. For a few days, we can recreate how boys and girls played, or go for a meal and a drink –beer with honey– in the tavern, the *thermopolium*, or in the restaurants that have Tarraco on the table, stroll through the mythology, laugh along with the popular theatre and comedy, listen to music or watch dancing, discover the tactics of the legionaries or attend a *pompa triumphalis*, which was the entrance into the city of a victorious general. To sum up, we can become Romans again for a few days. In summer the MHT also organises guided visits and concerts in the Roman city.

INTERNATIONAL FIREWORKS

During the first full week of July, every night the sky lights up with the international firework competition, the second biggest in the State, after that of San Sebastian, in the Basque Country, and where the biggest pyrotechnic companies in the world take part. The winner will be responsible for the firework display of Saint Thekla. The competition fills the whole city, but an inseparable image of it is that of the people on the El Miracle beach, eating while they wait for the firework display to begin.

GLORIOUS SAINT THEKLA

The festival of Saint Thekla, which is on the 23rd of September, sees Tarragona burst with life for ten days. It is the time to see the city in the street, in a festival that has been declared of national interest by the Generalitat, the Autonomous Government, and a state-wide festival of tourist interest, and which has a set of very well-ordered rituals. Tarragona's annual festival is one of the richest traditions in Catalonia, and the *Seguici Popular*, the most outstanding procession in both quantity and quality.

Although the celebration of Saint Thekla is earlier, the festival as it is known today originates in the 15th century when at the request of King Jaume II, on the 17th of May 1321, the relic of the saint's arm arrived in the city from Armenia. Greatly weakened during the 20th century, mainly due to the tourist policies of the 60s, the festival gained a new lease of life in democratic times, in the 80s, parallel to the rediscovery of the fire groups. In Tarragona, fantastic beasts have been known since the 14th century, when in 1381 the presence of the mythical *Cucafera* was witnessed.

As well as the *Ball de Diables*, the Beasts form part of the *Seguici Popular* (Dragon, Ox, the *Víbria* dragon, Eagle, Mule, *Cucafera*, Lion), the Magi of the Drums (named after the person who, in the 19th century, as today, came on horseback announcing the *Seguici*), the *Gegants* and *Nanos*, giants and bigheads (Giants of the city, Small Giants *Negrito* and *Negrita*, and Old Bigheads, all from the mid-19th century, and by the sculptor Bernat Verderol; Old Giants, from 1825, which bring the locals from the Cós del Bou district onto the street, and the *Nanos Nous*, new bigheads, which represent trades and entities in the city), the dances (*Ball de Bastons*, two groups; *Pastorets, Turcs i Cavallets, Patatuf, Cercolets, Gitanes, Valencians* and *Cossis*), the spoken dances (*Joan de Serrallonga* and *Dames i Vells*), and the allegorical representations (the Seven Deadly Sins and the *Moixiganga*, a short musical farce). The dance of *Dames i Vells* combines criticism of power with the war of the sexes and the generation gap, with the verbal clash between worn-out old men and lively young women.

The main areas for Saint Thekla are the Plaça de la Font, the Part Alta and the Rambla Nova, and the most heard and most sung music, the paso doble *Amparito Roca* by Jaume Teixidor.

The *Seguici* takes place on the 22nd and 23rd of September, Saint Thekla's Day. Summing up many of the festival events, we could say that the 20th is the day of the altarpiece of Saint Thekla, with scenes from her life in the Cathedral. The 21st, that of the opening speech, and the thunderclaps of fireworks that go with the *Arrencada Festiva* [the Festival Beginning], with the *Gegants*. The 22nd, that of the *Cercavila* [street parade] of Saint Thekla, with the *Seguici Popular* taking place before the Palau Municipal.

Saint Thekla's Day starts with the *Anada a Ofici*, with the *Seguici* accompanying the local authorities to the Cathedral Mass. At this mass the Joys of Saint Thekla are sung. After the mass, the *Seguici* participates again —as in all the events, with its musicians and strummers— in front of the City Hall. And at one o'clock, a much awaited moment: *Castells*, human towers, in the Plaça de la Font.

In the afternoon, *Anada a la Processó*, and a procession of the saint's relics in the Part Alta, with religious participation, unlike the morning's events. The entrance of the Arm, firstly in the *Pla de la Seu* and later, and above all, in the Cathedral, is a series of moments that is impossible to describe, with all the sections of the *Seguici* performing, the *colles castelleres*, human tower groups, doing *Vanos de Pilars*, a tower construction specially preserved in Tarragona, the Cathedral bells pealing, and a palm tree firework symbolising the palm of the martyrdom of Saint Thekla. A total explosion.

Afterwards, part of the *Seguici* goes down the Cathedral steps. The Giants dance like crazy in the Baixada de la Misericòrdia. The dance of the Moorish Giants with gypsy carriers is quite unforgettable. The gypsy community of the Part Alta is one of the most deeply-rooted in the city, and are largely responsible for the character of the old district. At night, the time has come for the Castell de Focs [firework castle] on the Miracle beach.

The festival of the Mercè, the 24th of September, is another great day for the human tower builders, with the *castellers*, the *pilars* of the four local groups, *colles*, making their way from the Plaça de les Cols to the balcony of the City Hall. It is also the day of the *Correfoc*, the firework parade, which goes along the Rambla Nova to the statue of the Despullats, where the devils, dragons and wild animals do a *carretillada* and fill the whole square with smoke and fire, with the so-called *wheelbarrows*. Everything, the festival, the fireworks and the events that we have not mentioned (concerts, dances) end with the strings of firecrackers, which are let off all along the Rambla Nova, from the Despullats to the Balcony.

CASTELLS

Saint Thekla closes the *casteller* season in Tarragona, one of the leading bases in this spectacular tradition, which from Camp de Tarragona and Penedès have extended throughout nearly all of Catalonia and beyond. The city has four groups or *colles*: the Xiquets de Tarragona, with white and red striped shirts; the Colla Jove dels Xiquets de Tarragona, lilac; the Xiquets del Serrallo, marine blue; and the Colla Castellera de Sant Pere i Sant Pau, which wears green shirts.

The *castells* first took shape towards the end of the 18th century or early 19th century as a development of interludes and older dances, such as the *Ball de Valencians*. The technique used turns them into a master work of fleeting architecture. To see them, and know how to value them, you have to concentrate on how many people form each storey, and how many storeys in height they reach. The formula to describe them starts with the number of people per storey (two, three, four...) and then the number of storeys (seven, eight, nine): four of eight, for example. A *castell* of one person per storey is a *pilar*, and the base made up of many is the *pinya*.

The *gralla*, wind instruments like flageolets, along with the drum, with the toc de *castells*, indicate that the construction is rising. A *castell* is completed, "loaded", when the *anxaneta*, a small boy or girl, crowns the tower and raises their arm, or as they say, *fa l'aleta* [flaps a wing]. Nobody applauds until then. The *castell* is "unloaded" when all the storeys have climbed down, and only the pinya remains in view. If a castell falls, *fa llenya*, it becomes firewood!

These are clearly the more general rules and there are others that you can learn by watching the events that are organised throughout the year, except in the heart of winter. An important event is the Concurs de Castells contest, which brings together some of the top level *colles*, which have achieved the tallest and most difficult *castells*, every two years on even numbers. It is held in the Plaça de Braus [Bullring] on the first Sunday of October. We could say, exaggerating but doing so without fear of erring, that they are the Olympic Games of the *castells*.

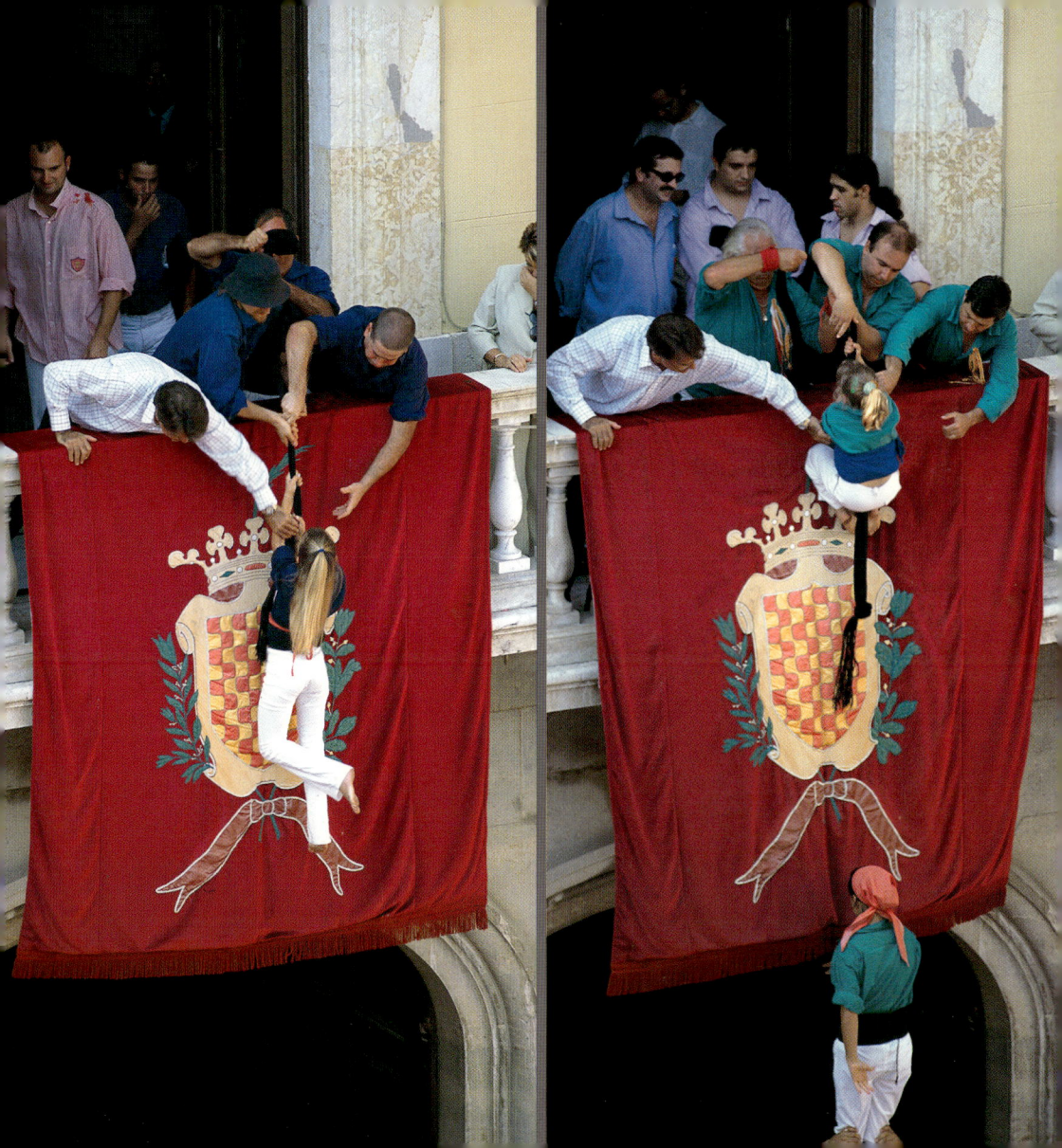

LA PLAÇA DE BRAUS, *where the two-yearly castells competition is held, is the work of the multifaceted Salas i Ricomà. It was built on a site previously occupied by a bastion, and Roman remains were found, such as a Roman milestone, which showed the distances on the roadside. It was opened in 1883 with two famous toreros, Frascuelo and Lagartijo.*

GASTRONOMY, ENOLOGY AND LEISURE

Gastronomy, enology —the Rovira i Virgili University has the first university faculty in the whole State in this speciality— and catering in Tarragona are nothing new. The historian Ludwig Friedlaender states that in the Lapidary Museum of Narbonne the plaque of a Roman freedman is conserved, "landlord of the Gallo tavern" in Tarragona. I wonder if the food was good there.

ROMESCO DE...

The king of cuisine in Tarragona is *romesco*, a name with different meanings. On the one hand, it is a ground mixture of seasoning that becomes a *suquet*, or gravy, when cooked with fish or meat. On the other hand, it is a sauce that is eaten cold, accompanying grilled fish, meat or vegetables, or to season salads. Some ingredients are essential, but others depend on the taste of the chef. And there are as many tastes as there are people who make *romesco*. To try and find the best a competition is held every two years on Saint Thekla's Day in El Serrallo, and the title of *mestre romescaire* is awarded. One of these maestros is David Solé, an excellent chef, both in practice, in the Restaurant Barquet, and in theory, as the author of books. He provides a recipe for romesco that *"might be the best, like any other"*:

"Fried romesco peppers (two), garlic (4 cloves), tomato (1 ripe), bread (1 fried slice), toasted hazelnuts (1/2 dozen), mature wine (1 dash), salt. Taking care not to burn the peppers, mix and chop everything together".

Romesco was a cheap meal that the fishermen cooked while on ship. Other more elaborate fish dishes were prepared at home. Some star dishes from Tarragona are the *rossejat* [rice stew] or golden noodles –not just any noodles!–, prawns, crayfish –here they are called *gadagang*–, stuffed cuttlefish, baby squid with onion, or specialities such as *groguillo*, a special sauce, *asmarris*, a fishermen's recipe, garlic and pepper, toasted garlic, omelette with cod… Many, such as rice with sardines, or anchovies with onion, have blue fish (sardines, tuna…) from Tarragona, protected by a quality guarantee.

CHARTREUSE, LONG LIFE

C hartreuse is the "national" drink of Tarragona. Although since 1989 it has only been produced in France, many people from Tarragona seek out bottles of Chartreuse produced here in bars, cafés and shops all over the world. This great liking has led to large private liquor collections being accumulated.

The formula for Chartreuse –there are two colours: yellow, milder, and green, stronger– is a secret. In 1605, a marshal gave the monks of the Monastery of Vauvert, in Paris, a manuscript with the formula for the Elixir of Long Life, of unknown origin. Màrius Serra has written the novel *Mon oncle*, the theme being the formula for this drink.

It is the base of the drink for the annual festival of Saint Thekla, *mamadeta*, a mixture of green and yellow Chartreuse and iced lemon. On the 21st of September, people from Tarragona take part in a mass Chartreuse tasting, in what is called "*Cafè, copa i puro per un duro*" [Coffee, a stiff drink and cigar for a *duro*, 5 pesetas], the price on offer before the arrival of the euro.

RTREUSE

FABRIQUÉE
CHARTREUSE

UR
G DE

L. Garnier

40º

PAR LES PÈRES CHARTREVX

E S.A.E. TARRAGONA (ESPAÑA)

CHARTR

LIQUEUR
A LA G DE

L. Garnier

55º

FABRIQUÉE PAR LES P

CHARTREUSE S.A.E. TAR

BIBLIOGRAPHY

Various authors, *Els balls parlats a la Catalunya Nova (Teatre popular català)*, Edicions El Mèdol, Tarragona, 1992.

Various authors, *Guia d'arquitectura del Camp*, Col·legi d'Arquitectes de Catalunya – Demarcació de Tarragona / Autoritat Portuària de Tarragona, Tarragona, 1995.

Various authors, *La ciutat pels carrers. 27 mirades sobre Tarragona*, Llibreria La Capona, Tarragona, 2002.

Various authors, *El llibre d'or de l'art català*. El Periódico, Barcelona, 1997.

Various authors, *Tàrraco. L'imperi a Catalunya*, Revista *Descobrir Catalunya*, number 9, April 1998.

Various authors, *Tarragona. El canvi de segle, 1890 – 1918*, Fundació Caixa de Pensions, Barcelona, 1986.

Various authors, *Tarragona. Territorio, historia, cultura y arte*. Energia e Industrias Aragonesas. Madrid, 1991.

Various authors, *Tarragona medieval*. Diari de Tarragona, Tarragona, 1999.

Various authors, *Tarragona poble a poble. Guia de les nostres comarques*. Diari de Tarragona, Tarragona, 2000.

Various authors, *Tarragona prehistórica. Los secretos del pasado*. Diari de Tarragona.

Various authors, *La Via Augusta. Vestigis de la Catalunya Romana*, Revista *Descobrir Catalunya*, number 69, October 2003.

ARBELOA I RIGAU, JOAN-VIANNEY M.; FARRÉ, JOAN; HAUSCHILD, THEODOR, *Tarragona romana*, Lunwerg Editores, Barcelona, 1993.

BAIXERAS, JOSEP A., *Fulls de calendari*, edition produced by Montserrat Palau, Fundació d'Estudis Socials Josep Recasens, Reus, 2003.

BARGALLÓ VALLS, JOSEP, *Els Pastorets de Tarragona, segons Els Pastorets de Josep Maria Folch i Torres*. Edicions El Mèdol, Tarragona, 2001.

BARGALLÓ VALLS, JOSEP; BERTRAN LUENGO, JORDI; FERRERES CATALÀ, SÍLVIA; MARTORELL COCA, JOSEP M. i LÓPEZ MONNÉ, RAFEL, *Tarragona. Guia de les festes de Santa Tecla. Història, seguici popular i castells*. Edicions El Mèdol, Tarragona, 1994.

BERTRAN, JORDI; GONZÁLEZ, XAVIER; MARTORELL, JOSEP M.; PRAT, JOAN; SUNYER, MAGÍ; LÓPEZ, RAFEL i JOVÉ, XAVIER, *El ball de diables de Tarragona. Teatre i festa a Catalunya*, Edicions El Mèdol, Tarragona, 1993.

CARANDELL, JOSEP M.; PÉREZ PUIGJANÉ, MANEL; ONTAÑÓN, FRANCISCO i LORRIO, FÉLIX, *Tarragona*, Lunwerg, Barcelona, 1989.

CARBONELL I BUADES, MARIÀ i GARRIGA I RIERA, JOAQUIM, *El Palau de la Generalitat a l'època del Renaixement*, Generalitat de Catalunya - Museu Nacional d'Art de Catalunya, Barcelona, 2004.

CARRERAS, JAUME i GARRIGA, ENRIC, *El Mèdol. Acta general d'un espai peculiar*. Edicions El Mèdol, Tarragona, 1992.

FRIEDLAENDER, LUDWIG, *La sociedad romana. Historia de las costumbres en Roma*, Fondo de Cultura Económica, Mèxic, 1947.

OLIVÉ, ENRIC; PIQUÉ, JORDI i RICOMÀ, F. XAVIER, *Tarragona. La imatge del temps*. Ajuntament de Tarragona, Tarragona 1990.

PALAU VERGÉS, MONTSERRAT; ET AL., *El llibre d'or de Catalunya. Un segle en imatges*, El Periódico, Barcelona, 1996.

WEBS

PERUCHO, JOAN. *Gastronomia i cultura*. Edicions El Mèdol, Tarragona, 1999.

PIN I SOLER, JOSEP, *Antologia tarragonina*, Institut d'Estudis Tarraconenses Ramon Berenguer IV, Diputació Provincial de Tarragona, Tarragona, 1992.

PUJALS, JOAN M., *Paisatges de Tarragona – Costa Daurada*, Lunwerg Editores, Barcelona, 1995.

RECASENS I COMES. JOSEP M., *La ciutat de Tarragona*, Editorial Barcino, Barcelona, 1966 (Volume I) i 1975 (Volume II).

REIAL SOCIETAT ARQUEOLÒGICA TARRACONENSE , *Tàrraco Patrimoni de la Humanitat*, Diari de Tarragona, Tarragona, 1998.

ROTA ALEU, JOSEP M.; ALEU VIÑAS, JOSEP M. i SANCHIS BERNABEU, MIQUEL, *Tarragona. Setmana Santa*, Edicions El Mèdol, Tarragona, 1999.

SERRA MASDEU, ANNA ISABEL, *Recorregut per la Tarragona modernista*, Edicions Cossetània, Valls, 2003.

SOLÉ I TORNÉ, DAVID, *Amb la mar al cor. La cuina a Tarragona*, Edicions El Mèdol, Tarragona, 1993.

VERGÉS, GERARD; GOMIS, RAMON i GUAL, JOSEP, *Barques i fogons. De Vinaròs a Calafell*, Edicions El Mèdol, Tarragona, 1990.

XIRINACS, OLGA, *Zona marítima*, Editorial Planeta, Barcelona, 1986.

Tarragona City Council:
http://www.tgna.org
http://www.ajtarragona.es
Associació Cultural Sant Fructuós:
http://www.acsantfructuos.org
Carnival of Tarragona:
http://www.carnavaltarragona.com
Chartreuse:
http://www.chartreuse.fr/pa_historia_liq_esp.htm
City Cave:
http://www.tinet.org/~tarraco/ztarracc1.html
Museu d'Art Modern de Tarragona:
http://www.altanet.org/MAMT
Museu Diocesà de Tarragona:
http://www.arquebisbattarragona.org/mdt
Museu d'Història de Tarragona:
http://www.museutgn.com
Museu Nacional Arqueològic de Tarragona:
http://www.mnat.es
Literary routes:
http://www.tarragonalletres.org/rutesliteraries.html
Universal Studios Port Aventura:
http://www.portaventura.es

Published by
TRIANGLE POSTALS, SL

Concept
JORDI PUIG · JOAN BARJAU

Text
© CARLES MARQUÈS, 2005

Photography
© RICARD PLA
JORDI PUIG
PERE VIVAS, 2005

Graphic design
JOAN BARJAU

Layout
VADOR MINOBIS

Translation
STEVE CEDAR

Production
IMMA PLANAS

Photomechanics
MOLAGRAF

Printed by
NG NIVELL GRÀFIC

Registration number
B: 36.118-2005

ISBN
84-8478-183-6

Acknowledgements to:
JOSEP BARGALLÓ
JORDI BERGADÀ
JORDI BERTRAN
CARLOS BLANCO
MAITE BLAY
MANEL BLAY
MERCÈ CAMERINO
ROSA COMES
JOSEP FONT
MARCELINA JANÉ
SOFIA MATA
MONTSERRAT MERCADÉ
MAGÍ MIRET
TOMÀS OLIVAR
MONTSERRAT PALAU
MERITXELL PÉREZ
DAVID SOLÉ
WALFRIDO STROHECKER
SALVADOR VECIANA
DOLORS VERGÉS

TRIANGLE POSTALS, SL
Sant Lluís, Menorca
Tel. +34 971 15 04 51
Fax +34 971 15 18 36
www.trianglepostals.com